Smithsonian

LITTLE EXPLORER

Water

by Martha E. H. Rustad

CAPSTONE PRESS
a capstone imprint

Little Explorer is published by Capstone Press,
1710 Roe Crest Drive, North Mankato, Minnesota 56003
www.capstonepub.com

**For Mom, for holding my hand and squeezing it
three times—MEHR**

Library of Congress Cataloging-in-Publication Data
Rustad, Martha E. H. (Martha Elizabeth Hillman), 1975–
  Water / by Martha E. H. Rustad.
     p. cm. — (Smithsonian Little explorer)
  Summary: "Introduces water and the water cycle to
young readers, including basic molecules, bodies of
water, water states, uses, and conservation"— Provided
by publisher.
  Audience: K to grade 3.
  Includes index.
  ISBN 978-1-4765-0249-6 (hardcover)
  ISBN 978-1-4765-3543-2 (paper over board)
  ISBN 978-1-4765-3549-4 (paperback)
  ISBN 978-1-4765-3555-5 (ebook PDF)
1. Water—Juvenile literature. 2. Hydrology—Juvenile
literature. 3. Hydrologic cycle—Juvenile literature.
I. Title.
GB848.R87 2014
 551.48—dc23   2012050590

Editorial Credits
Kristen Mohn, editor; Sarah Bennett, designer;
Marcie Spence, media researcher; Kathy McColley,
production specialist

Our very special thanks to Nancy Knowlton, Sant
Chair of Marine Sciences, National Museum of Natural
History, for her curatorial review. Capstone would also
like to thank Kealy Wilson, Smithsonian Institution
Project Coordinator and Product Development Manager,
and the following at Smithsonian Enterprises: Ellen
Nanney, Licensing Manager; Brigid Ferraro, Director
of Licensing; Carol LeBlanc, Senior Vice President,
Consumer & Education Products.

Image Credits
Alamy Images: Max McClure, 27 (bottom), Neil
Cooper, 27 (top left); Capstone: 12, 13 (right), 14 (top),
15 (right), 16 (top); Capstone Studio: Karon Dubke, 10,
14 (bottom), 22 (bottom left), 26 (front), 27 (top right);
Shutterstock: Adam Gilchrist, 8, Alan Bailey, 4 (bottom
left), Alena Ozerova, 15 (left), Anna Anisimova, 16
(bottom), Anteromite, 7 (top), Axily, 9 (top right), Blend
Images, (left), Brians, 4 (top left), Catalin Petolea, 17
(right), 21 (top), Chawalit S., 1, Creativa, 6 (bottom
right), Fudy Umans, 24 (top), gallimaufry, 22-23, Gerard
Koudenburg, 4 (right), Humannet, 30-31, 32, i3alda,
design element, Igor Kolos, 17 (left), Ilias Strachinis, 18
(middle), isak55, 26 (back), Jane September, 29 (bottom
right), john Michael evan potter, 23 (top), jonson,
cover, Josef Hanus, 18 (top), Juksy, design element,
Julian de Dios, 18 (bottom), kanate, 6-7, Kekyalyaynen,
25 (bottom), Konstantin Shishkin, 9 (left), Kozorez
Vladislav, 5 (bottom), Kozyrina Ogla, design element,
lobster20, 6 (bottom left), M. Unal Ozmenk, 11, (bottom),
Marcel Mooj, 28 (middle right), Maria Uspenskaya, 22
(top left), Mark Winfrey 24 (bottom), mikeledray, 2-3,
Patricia Marks, 29 (top left), Perspectives – Jeff smith, 19,
Photobac, 22 (top right), photobank.kiev.ua, 7 (bottom),
PhotoStock10, 28 (top right), risteski goce, 5 (top), Sadik
Gulec, 28 (bottom right), Sarunyu_foto, 9 (bottom right),
schankz, 4 (middle left), shao weiwei, 21 (bottom),
Stephan Bidouze, 25 (top), Stephen Bures, 29 (top right),
Steven Coling, 11 (top), Thomas M Perkins, 29 (bottom
left), Tomnamon, 28-29, ying, 20-21, yurly kulik, 13 (left)

Printed in the United States of America in Brainerd, Minnesota.
032013   007721BANGF13

TABLE OF CONTENTS

WE ALL NEED WATER

Water is wonderful. You can drink it,
wash with it, swim in it,
and ice skate on it!

People need water to live. Animals and plants need water too.

But what is water? Where does it come from?

The same water has been on Earth for billions of years.

Almost three-fourths of our planet is covered with water.

5

WHAT IS WATER?

Water is a clear liquid. It has no taste, smell, or color.

Tiny organisms live in every drop of water.

H₂O

Water is made up of teeny, tiny bits called molecules. Each molecule has two parts of hydrogen and one part of oxygen. Water can also be called H_2O.

There are about 326 million trillion gallons of water on Earth!

ICE

Water freezes into a solid when it is cold. When water turns into ice, it expands.

Water freezes at 32 degrees Fahrenheit (0 degrees Celsius).

Ice cubes float on the water in your glass.

Layers of ice float in a lake.

Icebergs float
in the ocean.

TRY THIS!

Ask an adult for help.

Find a clear plastic container.

Make a line on the side
with tape or a crayon.

Fill it up to the line with water.

Put it in the freezer overnight.

Where is the ice?
Where is your line?

GAS

Heat makes water molecules move
fast and create bubbles. It turns the
water into a gas that floats away.

The water seems to disappear.
But it has only evaporated.
It has become part of the air.

Water boils at 212 degrees Fahrenheit (100 degrees Celsius).

TRY THIS!

Ask an adult for help.

Find a clear glass container.

Make a line on the side with tape or a crayon.

Fill it up to the line with water.

Put it in a microwave on high for 4 minutes.

Where is the water? Where is the line?

THE WATER CYCLE

The water cycle moves water around the planet. Water goes from the ground to the sky and back again.

Earth doesn't make new water. It recycles the same water again and again.

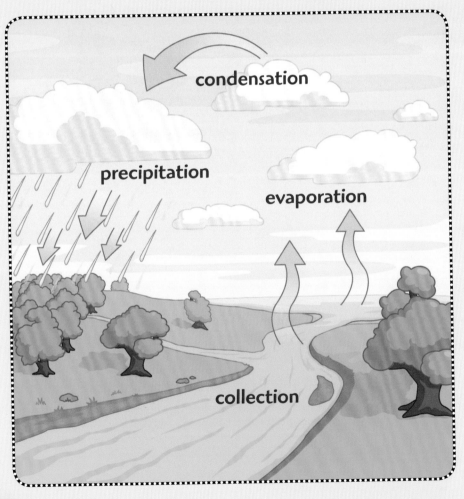

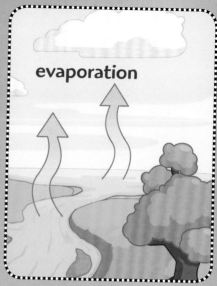
evaporation

EVAPORATION

The sun heats water in oceans, lakes, rivers, and even puddles.

Heated water evaporates from bodies of water.

It turns into a gas called vapor. Water vapor rises into the air.

condensation

CONDENSATION

In the sky, cool air condenses warm water vapor.

The gas turns back into a liquid. Water droplets gather to make clouds.

The droplets in the clouds grow and become heavy.

precipitation

PRECIPITATION

Water drops back down to the ground.

Rain is a kind of precipitation. Snow, sleet, and hail are also precipitation.

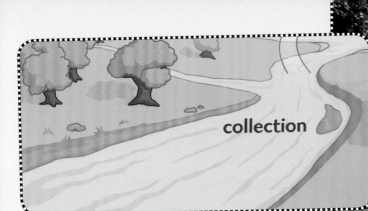
collection

COLLECTION

Gravity pulls precipitation to the ground. It soaks into tiny spaces between dirt and rocks.

Water gathers in rivers, lakes, and oceans.

Sunlight heats the bodies of water. The water cycle begins again.

Gravity is a force that pulls things toward the center of Earth. Jump up. Gravity is what brings you back down.

Water that flows deep underground is called groundwater. People dig wells to reach groundwater for drinking.

BODIES OF WATER

We see moving water in rivers and streams.

We see still water in lakes and ponds.

At the North and South Poles some water is frozen in ice sheets and glaciers.

Glaciers formed thousands of years ago from deep snow that piled up in valleys. It turned into ice.

But rivers, lakes, and glaciers make up
only a small part of the world's water.

Nearly all the water on Earth
is in the oceans.

Bodies of Water	How much of the world's water?
oceans	97%
frozen at poles	2%
rivers, lakes, and groundwater	1%

SALT WATER

Rainwater that falls from clouds is not salty. Yet most of the water on Earth is salt water.

Groundwater moves through the ground on its way to the oceans.

Tiny bits of minerals become trapped in it. This makes ocean water salty.

Freshwater in lakes, streams, and rivers does not have salt.

Salt must be taken out of ocean water before people can drink it. Factories remove salt from seawater in many places around the world.

When ocean water evaporates, salt is left behind. When ocean water freezes, most of the salt is left behind. Some ice in the ocean is a little salty.

USES OF WATER

We use water for drinking and cooking. We use water to stay clean.

Farmers use water to make food. Water helps crops grow. Farm animals drink water.

About 50 glasses of water are needed to grow enough oranges to make one glass of orange juice!

In the United States, out of every 100 gallons of water ...
power plants use 48 gallons
farms use 36 gallons
people use 11 gallons
factories use 5 gallons

People use water to make power. Dams capture energy from moving water. Power plants turn the energy into electricity.

WATER POLLUTION

We sometimes pollute our water.

Many farms use chemicals
to keep bugs off crops.
The chemicals can wash
into groundwater.

Factories might dump
waste into rivers.

People sometimes drop garbage in lakes. Garbage and chemicals from the land are often carried to the ocean.

We should work to keep our water clean. It's the only water we have.

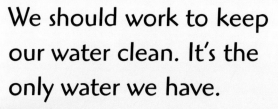

WATER TREATMENT PLANTS
Dirty water goes down the drain. Water treatment plants use machines and chemicals to clean the water. The plants pump clean water into large tanks. People use the water again.

DRINKING WATER

Our bodies need water. We get some water from the food we eat.

Our bodies are about 60 percent water.

We need about eight glasses of water each day to stay healthy.

WHERE DOES YOUR WATER COME FROM?

Turn on the tap. Water flows out. Pipes carry water to my house.

Pull up and down on the pump handle. My water runs out of a well.

Pick up a bucket. Go to the river. Water flows into my bucket.

CONSERVATION

People should conserve water.
Use only as much as you need.

According to the Environmental Protection
Agency, an American family of four uses
an average of 400 gallons (1,514 liters) of
water every day!

We share water with
everyone in the
world. We also share
water with people
in the future.

The same water keeps going around and around planet Earth.

Everyone needs water.

GLOSSARY

condense—to change from gas to liquid

conserve—to protect something from being wasted or lost

dam—a barrier built across a river or stream to hold back water

evaporate—to change from a liquid into a gas

gas—a form of matter that is not solid or liquid; it can move about freely and does not have a definite shape

hydrogen—a colorless gas that is lighter than air

liquid—a wet substance that can be poured

mineral—a solid found in nature that has a crystal structure

molecule—the atoms making up the smallest unit of a substance; H_2O is a molecule of water

organism—a living plant or animal

oxygen—a colorless gas in the air that people and other animals need to breathe

pollute—to make something dirty or unsafe

precipitation—all forms of water that fall from clouds

solid—something that holds its shape; not a liquid or a gas

water vapor—water in the form of a gas; water vapor is tiny bits of water that cannot always be seen

well—a deep hole in the ground that is made to get water, oil, or natural gas

CRITICAL THINKING USING THE COMMON CORE

Name three types of precipitation. How are they alike and different? Describe them using details from the text. (Key Ideas and Details)

On page 12 the author says, "Earth doesn't make new water. It recycles the same water again and again." What does the author mean by this? (Craft and Structure)

Look at the molecule diagram on page 7. Explain what the H and O represent. Why are there two Hs and one O? (Integration of Knowledge and Ideas)

READ MORE

Hammersmith, Craig. *The Water Cycle.* Earth and Space Science. Mankato, Minn.: Capstone Press, 2012.

Lyon, George Ella. *All the Water in the World.* New York: Atheneum Books for Young Readers, 2011.

Masters, Nancy R. *How Did that Get to My House? Water.* Community Connections. Ann Arbor, Mich.: Cherry Lake Pub., 2010.

INTERNET SITES

FactHound offers a safe, fun way to find Internet sites related to this book. All of the sites on FactHound have been researched by our staff.

Here's all you do:

Visit www.facthound.com

Type in this code: 9781476502496

 Check out projects, games and lots more at
www.capstonekids.com

INDEX